Levi Strauss

History Maker Bios

Stephanie Sammartino McPherson

LERNER PUBLICATIONS COMPANY • MINNEAPOLIS

For my daughter Jennifer, a constant source of joy and inspiration

The author wishes to thank Lynn Downey, historian of Levi Strauss & Co., for carefully reading the manuscript for accuracy. She also thanks her editor, Sara Hoffmann, for her support and valuable suggestions, and Richard McPherson and Marion and Angelo Sammartino for their usual encouragement and helpful comments.

In 1906, an earthquake and fire in San Francisco destroyed the headquarters of Levi Strauss & Co. The records of Levi Strauss's life were also lost. Because of this, many legends have grown up about him. This book presents only what we know for certain about Levi Strauss.

Illustrations by Big Time Attic

Text copyright © 2007 by Stephanie Sammartino McPherson
Illustrations copyright © 2007 by Lerner Publications Company

Lerner Publications Company
A division of Lerner Publishing Group
241 First Avenue North
Minneapolis, MN 55401 U.S.A.

Website address: www.lernerbooks.com

Library of Congress Cataloging-in-Publication Data

McPherson, Stephanie Sammartino.
    Levi Strauss / Stephanie Sammartino McPherson.
        p.   cm. — (History maker bios)
    Includes bibliographical references and index.
    ISBN-13: 978-0-8225-6581-9 (lib. bdg. : alk. paper)
    ISBN-10: 0-8225-6581-1 (lib. bdg. : alk. paper)
        1. Strauss, Levi, 1829–1902—Juvenile literature. 2. Levi Strauss and
    Company—History—Juvenile literature. 3. Businesspeople—United States—
    Biography—Juvenile literature. 4. Clothing trade—United States—History—
    Juvenile literature. 5. Jeans (Clothing)—History—Juvenile literature. I. Title.
    II. Series.
    HD9940.U4S7973 2007
    338.7'687113092—dc22   2006008152

Manufactured in the United States of America
1 2 3 4 5 6 – JR – 12 11 10 09 08 07

TABLE OF CONTENTS

INTRODUCTION

Levi Strauss had a head for business. He loved buying and selling. He also wanted to make a better life for himself. In 1853, Levi headed west. A man named James Marshall had discovered gold in California. Adventurers from all around the country hurried to California to make their fortunes.

Levi didn't look for gold. But he did strike it rich. He opened a business that sold goods to small shops. Later, he made and sold sturdy pants. Levi became one of the most important people in San Francisco. His company grew bigger than he ever imagined. Levi used his wealth to help make the city a better place for everyone.

This is his story.

1 YOUNG LEVI

On February 26, 1829, Hirsch and Rebecca Strauss welcomed a baby boy into the world. It would be many years before anyone called him Levi. The happy parents named their new son Loeb.

The Strauss family was Jewish. They lived in the town of Buttenheim. Buttenheim was in a part of Germany called Bavaria. But Bavaria was never much of a home to the Strausses. Loeb could not remember a time when Jews had the same rights as other Germans. Laws limited the jobs that Jews could hold. Other laws forced them to live in certain areas. Loeb could not hope for a very good life in Bavaria.

Hirsch and Rebecca Strauss's home in Buttenheim, Bavaria

Loeb grew up in Bavaria, Germany (ABOVE). As a Jewish family in Germany in the 1800s, the Strausses were treated unfairly.

Many Jewish families left Bavaria to come to the United States. The Strauss family might have left too. But Loeb's father, Hirsch, became ill. He had a lung disease called tuberculosis.

Hirsch was worn out from hard work and worry. He had a large family to support. He had five children from his first marriage. After his first wife died, Hirsch had married Rebecca. Besides his half brothers and sisters, Loeb had an older sister named Vogela.

Loeb's father died in 1845. The Strauss family no longer had a reason to stay in Bavaria. In the United States, they would have more freedom. They could have a better future too. Within two years, Loeb, his mother, and his half sister Mathilde were ready to leave for the United States. Vogela may have joined them on their journey.

Like the Strausses, these immigrants set sail for the United States in the 1800s. They left their homes in search of better lives.

Sailing across the ocean in 1847 was a hardship. The Strauss family could not afford to travel first class. Instead, they shared a stuffy room with dozens of other passengers. The food was bad. The beds were hard and narrow. The passengers were often seasick. Only the thought of a fresh start in the United States made the trip bearable.

Ships carrying immigrants were crowded and uncomfortable.

Many immigrants arrived in New York in the mid-1800s.

Luckily, the Strausses were not alone when they arrived at their new home. Loeb's half brothers, Jonas and Louis, had come to New York earlier. They welcomed their family to the noisy, bustling city. Jonas and Louis had already set up a wholesale business. Wholesale businesses sell goods to stores. Then the stores sell them to customers.

It seemed natural for Loeb to work with his brothers. He was eager to learn and succeed. In the United States, it didn't matter where you were born or what religion you practiced. What did matter was how hard you were willing to work. Loeb didn't mind hard work and long hours. He would do whatever it took to get ahead.

COUNTRY PEDDLER?

One story says that Loeb spent several years in Kentucky peddling goods from door-to-door. Loeb was certainly strong enough to carry a pack full of goods to sell. And he was healthy enough to walk ten miles a day, as peddlers often had to do. Historians don't know if this story is true. But they do know that Loeb loved business and was a quick learner.

Levi's brothers purchased goods for their customers to buy. Wholesalers often bought goods on New York's busy docks (ABOVE).

Soon Loeb was dealing with customers. It was a good way to learn English. He began to call himself Levi. Perhaps he thought it was easier to say. Or maybe he thought it sounded more American. The determined young man had a new name to match his new country.

2 GOLD FEVER

Something exciting happened soon after Levi came to the United States. He heard rumors of a discovery in California. More and more reports reached New York. The rumors were true! The mountains in northern California were full of gold.

Newspapers spread the word. "Fortune lies upon . . . the earth as plentiful as the mud in our streets," wrote a journalist named Horace Greeley.

Soon the whole nation had gold fever. Thousands of young men left home to search for gold. Some sailed to California in boats. Others headed west in covered wagons. By the middle of 1849, thousands of covered wagons were creaking slowly across the prairies.

Wagon trains heading to California had to cross the steep, dangerous Rocky Mountains.

Levi listened to tales of the gold rush. The stories were fascinating. But Levi was busy with his work. And he was still learning new customs and a new language. It was not the right time to make another new start. Besides, Levi was a businessperson. He liked what he did. He could not see himself as a gold miner.

SOMETHING SHINY

James Marshall was in charge of building a machine called a mill for a ranch near San Francisco. The mill was supposed to provide wood for the ranch. But on January 24, 1848, something shiny caught James's eye. It was a small pebble lying at the bottom of a shallow canal. James believed he had discovered gold. His boss, John Sutter, did some simple tests. The tests proved that the pebbles did contain gold. John's mill was never finished. His workers left to seek gold.

Gold miners at work in California

Yet thoughts of California excited Levi. Boatloads of people were arriving in San Francisco, a city on California's coast. Some set off for the gold fields. Others stayed in the wild, western town. These people would need all sorts of things.

San Francisco was full of business opportunities. Levi decided it was just the place for him. Levi's brothers agreed. Levi could find customers for their business in California.

In 1853, Levi became a U.S. citizen. At last, the time was right for him to make a big move. Levi set out on another ocean voyage.

Levi's second trip was hard. He sailed all the way to Panama before traveling to San Francisco. That was how most people got to California back then. But Levi was looking forward to his new life. He had many exciting plans. He hoped to start a business of his own.

3 GROWING BUSINESS

Levi didn't go far once he reached land. He rented space near a wharf. Ships stop at wharves. The ships carried supplies. Levi bought lots of supplies. He planned to sell these supplies to others.

Levi soon opened his own wholesale business. He called the business Levi Strauss. Ships began dropping off goods especially for Levi. Levi took these goods into his warehouse. Then he sent them to stores across the West Coast. Stores would wait to get goods from Levi. They bought many things from him.

All kinds of goods arrived at the wharves in San Francisco from the eastern United States. Lumber and other goods arrived on the Stewart Street Wharf.

New stores crowded
San Francisco's streets
in the mid-1800s.

More and more people
started opening stores in San Francisco.
These people needed goods to sell to their
customers. Many of the people bought
goods from Levi's business. They were
willing to pay very high prices. A blanket
that cost five dollars in New York might sell
for forty dollars in San Francisco. Levi
began to make a lot of money. His new
business was doing well.

Fanny came to San Francisco in 1856. By that time, the city was already very busy.

In 1856, Levi's sister Vogela came to San Francisco. Like Levi, she had changed her name when she moved to the United States. People called her Fanny.

She had also gotten married. Fanny's husband, David Stern, came with her to the city. Soon David joined Levi in business. The two men became partners.

Levi's brothers in New York sent him items to sell. Levi looked forward to their shipments of clothes, umbrellas, and other things. But Levi did more than anyone to make the business a success. He made sure he had what customers wanted. He always priced his goods fairly.

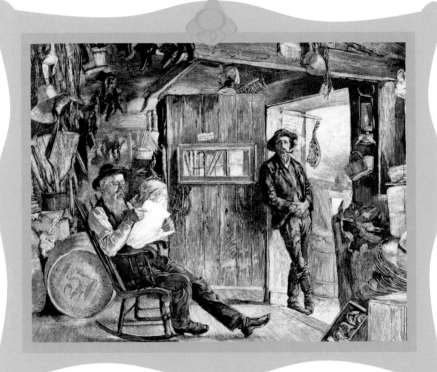

Stores around the region sold Levi's goods. Wholesalers supplied store owners with clothing, hats, household goods, and other items.

Levi's business continued to thrive. The company grew bigger and bigger. As the business expanded, Levi moved into larger buildings. Soon Levi changed the name of the business too. He decided to call it Levi Strauss & Co.

Shortage of Cotton

The U.S. Civil War (1861–1865) was far from California. But the war years were hard for California merchants like Levi. Levi sold cotton goods. Cotton grew in the South, where soldiers were fighting. Fewer cotton goods were available during the war. But Levi kept his business running.

Wagon drivers carried cotton to market in the 1800s. But when the Civil War began, cotton was hard to come by.

Soldiers from the North and South fought each other during the U.S. Civil War.

Levi's business opened early in the morning. It closed late at night. Levi did not have much time for himself. That may be why he never married. He might have been too busy to look for a wife. But Levi was not lonely. He lived with his sister Fanny and her family. Fanny had seven children. Levi came to love them as though they were his own.

San Francisco has many synagogues, but that wasn't always the case. Levi Strauss helped support the city's first synagogue, Temple Emanu-El (LEFT).

Levi was beginning to feel at home in San Francisco. He was interested in everything that happened there. He gave money to support the first Jewish synagogue. A synagogue is a Jewish place of worship. Levi was happy to live in a city where Jews could practice their religion. He wanted to help others of all faiths. He supported orphanages and other charities. He was known for his kindness.

In 1866, Levi moved his headquarters to one of San Francisco's main streets. By this time, many men worked for him. The new building was large. It had a big elevator and fancy lights. It also had a showroom. Merchants looked over the goods in the showroom. Then they chose what they wanted to sell in their stores. The company name was carved above the doorway. Levi Strauss & Co. was known all over the city.

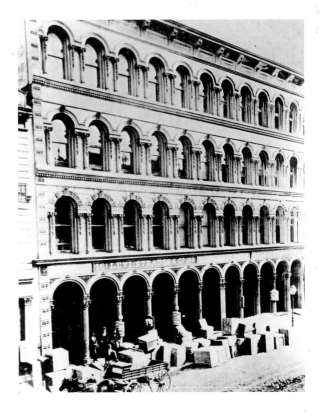

Levi's new company headquarters was big and fancy. The building had enough room for the company's many workers.

4 A NEW KIND OF PANTS

In 1872, Levi got a letter that changed his company forever. The letter came from a tailor in Reno, Nevada. The tailor's name was Jacob Davis.

Levi read Jacob's letter carefully. The tailor had an interesting tale to tell. He had invented a new way to make pants. Almost everyone wanted a pair. Jacob could not make the pants fast enough.

What made the pants special were rivets. Jacob used these small metal bolts to fasten pockets onto the pants. The rivets kept the pockets from ripping off. A miner could stuff such pockets with rocks and tools. Levi thought this was a very clever idea.

As Strong as a Horse Blanket

Jacob Davis first used rivets for horse blankets—not pants. The rivets held sturdy straps onto the blankets. One day, a woman needed some big, strong pants. She said her husband's pants were always wearing out. Jacob's horse blankets lasted a long time. He hoped that the rivets would make pants last longer too!

Jacob Davis was
a customer of
Levi Strauss & Co.
He bought cloth
from the business.

But Jacob had a problem. His fellow
tailors were jealous of his success. Jacob
feared they would steal his idea. If
everyone started making pants with rivets,
Jacob would not make much money. He
wanted to patent his invention. That meant
Jacob would be the only person allowed to
sell pants with rivets.

Jacob needed a business partner. He
knew that Levi was successful and honest.
He decided to ask Levi to be his partner.

Levi agreed to Jacob's plan. He wanted to sell pants with rivets. He knew the pants would make him lots of money.

On May 20, 1873, Levi and Jacob got their patent. Levi Strauss & Co. became more than a wholesale business. The company started making a product of its own. Levi was in charge of selling the pants. Jacob's job was to make the clothing. Jacob started a small factory. He hired women to run the sewing machines.

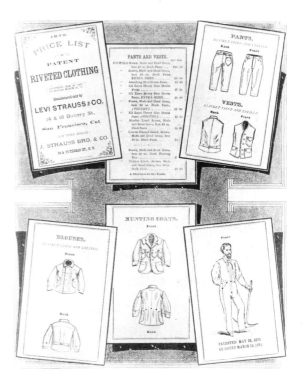

Levi got his first patent in 1873. His company went on to patent many other products. These patents were given to the company in 1879.

Levi and Jacob used denim to make their pants. Denim was a popular fabric. It was strong and comfortable. The men especially liked blue denim. Blue pants would not show many stains.

By this time, the gold rush had ended. But there were still miners who needed sturdy pants. Cowboys, lumberjacks, and farmers wanted them too. By the end of the year, Levi and Jacob had sold thousands of pants.

Strong denim pants were popular with miners, who spent long hours doing hard and dirty work.

Levi was happy with his success. But then something terrible happened. His brother-in-law David Stern died on January 2, 1874. Levi had lived with his sister and David for many years. He grieved deeply.

One year later, Fanny married her brother-in-law, William Sahlein. William was a widower with one child. Fanny's house was too small for her new, larger family. Her husband bought a bigger house. There was plenty of room for Levi.

Levi lived with Fanny and William in San Francisco.

By the 1870s, California was bustling with people and businesses.

Levi had lots of interests outside his company. He helped to direct a bank. He was also a director of a large utility company. This company supplied gas and electricity to many homes and businesses in California. Levi was very active in his community. He was an important person in the city of San Francisco.

San Francisco continued to grow. And Levi continued to make lots of money. In 1875, Levi and two of his friends bought the Mission and Pacific Woolen Mills. This business made blankets and fabric. Levi had been buying fabric from the mills for years. He used it to line his clothing. When Levi bought the mill, he got his very own supply of fabric.

Levi Strauss & Co. used a lot of fabric to make its earliest pairs of pants.

Levi wanted a logo for his popular pants. He hoped that this special design would remind people how strong his pants were. Someone came up with the idea of horses. The new logo showed two horses trying to pull apart a pair of Levi's pants. But the pants would not rip. In 1886, the company began sewing leather patches with the logo onto its pants.

Businesses use logos to help sell their products. Levi Strauss & Co. used its logo to sell more pants.

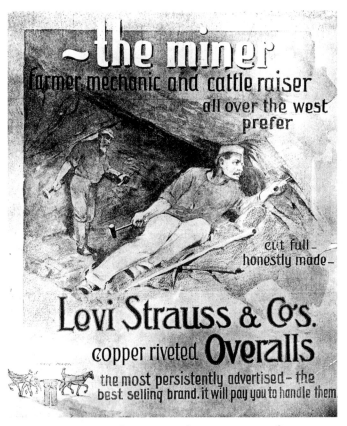

the miner

farmer, mechanic and cattle raiser all over the west prefer

cut full — honestly made —

Levi Strauss & Co's. copper riveted Overalls

the most persistently advertised — the best selling brand. it will pay you to handle them.

Levi Strauss & Co. ran advertisements for its clothing. This ad shows workers wearing Levi's denim pants.

Levi made a promise to go with his new logo. He said that he would replace any ripped pants with a brand-new pair. Levi believed his pants were very strong. And he was right! Few people ever asked Levi for a new pair of pants.

5 LEADING CITIZEN

Levi didn't dress in denim pants. He wore formal, black suits. He also liked to wear a shiny top hat. But Levi wasn't formal when it came to greeting people. He told all his workers to call him by his first name.

By the late 1880s, Levi had more than five hundred people working for him. He had a big, fancy office. But he liked to spend time in his factory and warehouse. One reporter wrote that Levi "prefers to do his talking while leaning against a pile of blankets out in the storerooms."

Many people worked at Levi Strauss & Co. These workers are making overalls for the company.

Levi loved his work. "I've been in the [business] for forty-three years," he said in 1895. "I could not live without my daily duties. . . . My happiness lies in my routine work." But Levi did not believe that money could buy happiness.

Levi found true happiness in his family and friendships. He continued to give money to many charities. He also wanted to help young people go to school.

Levi helped poor students attend the University of California (ABOVE).

Levi had not attended college. But he valued education. He thought it was important to work hard and learn new things. In 1897, Levi gave some money to the University of California. The school used the money to help students who could not afford to pay for college on their own.

LEVI'S SURPRISE

One night, Levi came home to a delightful surprise. Twenty-eight students were waiting to greet him. They were able to attend college because of Levi's gift to the University of California. The students gave Levi an album that held a special thank-you letter. They told Levi how grateful they were for their education. They also told Levi how much they admired him.

As Levi grew older, he began to give his nephews more control of the business. He continued to help his community. But he was aging. Levi's beard turned white. He had heart problems. He kept on working, but his health was failing.

On September 26, 1902, Levi died. Everyone in San Francisco felt sad. Businesses closed so their owners could attend his funeral.

All his life, Levi worked hard and helped his community. Many people admired him.

Levi left his company to his four nephews. But he left his example of fairness and generosity to the whole city. People respected Levi for his success. They loved him for his kindness and good deeds.

TIMELINE

In the year . . .

1847 Levi immigrated to the United States.   Age 18

1848 James Marshall discovered gold in
California.

1849 Levi changed his name from Loeb to Levi.

1853 he became a U.S. citizen.   Age 24
he traveled by ship from New York to
California.
he established a wholesale business in San
Francisco.

1856 his brother-in-law David Stern joined the
business.

1863 Levi renamed the business Levi Strauss & Co.

1866 the company moved to fancy headquarters
in the heart of the city.

1872 Levi received a letter from tailor Jacob
Davis.

1873 Levi and Jacob received a patent for riveted   Age 44
pants.

1875 Levi and two friends bought the Mission
and Pacific Woolen Mills.

1897 he established twenty-eight scholarships at   Age 68
the University of California at Berkeley.

1902 he died on September 26.   Age 73

1906 an earthquake and fire destroyed the
headquarters of Levi Strauss & Co.

1928 the company began calling its pants Levi's.

44

Jeans across the Nation

Levi Strauss's company continued to grow after his death. Cowboys and workers in the West bought more riveted overalls than any other type of pants. When World War II (1939–1945) began, the government limited the amount of metal the company could use. The company could not get as much fabric either. Strong pants were in great demand. There were not enough to go around.

After the war, Levi's pants became popular across the nation. They weren't just for workers anymore. Young people especially loved to wear denim pants. They began calling them jeans.

The company wanted people to know how special their pants were. They did not want their jeans confused with any others. In 1928, they began calling their jeans Levi's. Later, the company adopted a motto that Levi Strauss would have liked: "Everyone knows his first name."

FURTHER READING

NONFICTION

Kalman, Bobbie. *The Life of a Miner.* **New York: Crabtree Publishing Company, 2000.** Learn all about mining in this fun book.

Peterson, Tiffany. *Levi Strauss.* **Chicago: Heinemann Library, 2003.** This biography tells about Levi Strauss and his company.

Sutcliffe, Jane. *Milton Hershey.* **Minneapolis: Lerner Publications Company, 2004.** Read about the life of Milton Hershey—another famous American businessperson.

FICTION

Fleischman, Sid. *By the Great Horn Spoon!* **1963. Reprinted, Boston: Little, Brown, 1988.** This chapter book tells the story of Jack's trip to California and his adventures seeking gold.

Levitin, Sonia. *Boom Town.* **New York: Orchard Books, 1998.** Like Levi Strauss, Amanda strikes it rich in California without panning for gold. She sells gooseberry pies to the miners.